W9-BLS-340

INHALANT, WHIPPET, AND POPPER ABUSE

CAROLYN DECARLO

Rosen
YA
New York

Published in 2019 by The Rosen Publishing Group, Inc.
29 East 21st Street, New York, NY 10010

Copyright © 2019 by The Rosen Publishing Group, Inc.

First Edition

Library of Congress Cataloging-in-Publication Data

Names: DeCarlo, Carolyn, author.
Title: Inhalant, whippet, and popper abuse / Carolyn DeCarlo.
Description: New York : Rosen Publishing, 2019 | Series: Overcoming addiction |
Audience: Grades 7–12. | Includes bibliographical references and index.
Identifiers: ISBN 9781508179450 (library bound) | ISBN 9781508179610 (pbk.)
Subjects: LCSH: Inhalant abuse—Juvenile literature. | Drug abuse—Juvenile literature.
Classification: LCC HV5822.S65 D43 2019 | DDC 362.29'93--dc23

Manufactured in the United States of America

CONTENTS

INTRODUCTION

While some categories of drugs seem to get a lot of attention in the media and antidrug campaigns, inhalants are often looked over for their addictive properties. In fact, whereas you would be hard pressed to find a person alive today who does not know that heroin is an illegal drug, many people who don't abuse inhalants would not even know about the non-traditional uses of these chemicals to get high.

As you might have guessed, the term "inhalants" is fairly self-explanatory. Inhalants can be defined as "substances that people typically take only by inhaling." They are divided into three categories: aliphatic, aromatic, or halogenated hydrocarbons; nitrous oxide; and volatile alkyl nitrates. People take inhalants in a variety of ways, including sniffing or snorting the fumes; "dusting," or spraying aerosols directly into the nose or mouth; "huffing," or using a chemical-soaked rag to reach a quick high; "bagging," or spraying chemicals into a paper or plastic bag; inhaling nitrous oxide (i.e., "laughing gas") from balloons; and "glading" from air freshener aerosols. Huffing and bagging are the preferred methods of inhaling, as they allow greater concentrations of inhalants into the body.

Inhalants are derived from four main sources: solvents (liquids that become gas at air temperature), aerosol sprays, gases, and nitrites. Volatile solvents include household products such as paint thinner, gasoline, felt-tip markers, nail polish remover, and glue, as well as others. Aerosol sprays are the result of a solvent plus a propellant, such as spray paint, deodorant, and some hair care products. The most common "gas" inhalant is nitrous oxide, also known as laughing gas.

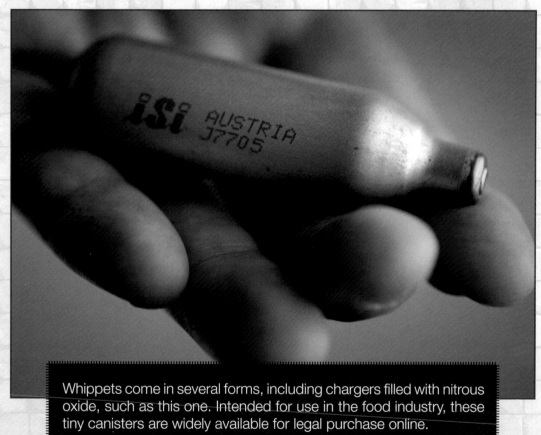

Whippets come in several forms, including chargers filled with nitrous oxide, such as this one. Intended for use in the food industry, these tiny canisters are widely available for legal purchase online.

"Whippets" refer primarily to whipped cream aerosols or dispensers; "Whip-It" is a brand of compressed nitrous oxide tanks sold semi-legally in head shops and on the internet. "Poppers" are amyl nitrites, a group of chemicals used and sold legally in room odorizers in the United States. Called "little bottled headaches," they are headache-inducing but used for a specific, desired effect, which is to loosen up involuntary muscles (otherwise known as smooth muscle tissue) in the throat and anus, and for a boost in sex drive. Poppers are more often abused by adults and those seeking sexual enhancement over euphoria. Much like bath salts and salvia, whippets and poppers are sometimes-legal psychoactive (mind-altering) substances that trend in and out of drug culture as party favorites.

As suggested above, inhalants are often made from products easily purchased in supermarkets, such as spray paints, markers, glues, and cleaning fluids. These products aren't intended for getting high, so they are not typically seen as "drugs," although they have psychoactive properties. These products are selected for their low price, legality, widespread availability, and rapid highs, and as such they are the only class of substance more often used by younger than older teens. Inhalants are especially common in minority populations and lower economic classes, and correlate with social determinants of health.

CHAPTER 1

HISTORY

Despite the fact that most inhalants can be found in modern household cleaning products and other everyday chemicals, their discovery predates the modern science lab. Detection of these chemicals and their properties can be traced back several centuries, with their primary uses varying wildly over the decades.

A quick search under the kitchen sink in any US household would likely turn up a selection of products that are used for huffing.

FROM THE HOSPITAL WARD TO THE DANCE FLOOR

The first use of amyl nitrite can be traced back to a Scottish physician named Lauder Brunton, who used it to treat a heart condition called angina pectoris in the 1800s. Angina pectoris occurs when there is not enough blood flow to the heart, and amyl nitrite helps by opening arteries to improve blood flow. The drug was packaged in small glass vials, which were crushed between the thumb and fingers so the vapors could be inhaled. The vials of amyl nitrite became known as "poppers" because they made a small popping sound when crushed.

Advances in medicine in the 1960s led to soldiers using them during the Vietnam War. The drug was rebranded as an antidote to cyanide poisoning from chemical weapons and gun fumes—but was more likely used as a cheap and legal high. When the soldiers returned from war, they found amyl nitrites had been downgraded to over-the-counter drugs, making them even more widely available. Throughout the '60s, amyl nitrites were used without any regulation, until the Food and Drug Administration (FDA) labeled them a prescription-only drug in 1969. From that point on, manufacturers evaded this law by using slightly altered formulas—butyl nitrite and isobutyl nitrite—which did not require FDA approval because they were not marketed as either drugs or food.

After the mafia became involved in the business of selling poppers, the drug underwent a rebrand as semi-legal room odorizers. At the same time, large advertising campaigns were launched in the media suggesting that poppers have intrinsically sex-enhancing properties. By 1974, poppers had gained a lot of popularity, particularly in gay bars and clubs. It was only ther that any actual health effects started to come to light, including drops in blood pressure, less blood to the brain, dizziness and nausea.

THE WHIP-IT! BRAND

The Whip-It! whipped cream chargers were first developed by the brand's original factories in Switzerland in the 1940s. Today, these chargers, filled with nitrous oxide gas, sell online in cases of up to six hundred. As the most popular manufacturer of these chargers, the company attributes its continued success to "an increase in coffee consumption, for which whipping cream is increasingly used to substitute aerosolized cans of whipped cream."

However, Whip-It! is not the only brand that sells chargers and dispensers. Some other brands of nitrous oxide chargers available for sale include ISI, Cafe Creme, Creme 24, EZ Whip, Gourmet, BestWhip Mr. Creamy, Liss, PureWhip, and EasyWhippets. Chefs may indeed use these chargers for their intended purpose, but drug users are also abusing them as a source of nitrous oxide. Recent studies show that whippets have become the most popular inhalant in use, with more than twelve million users in the United States who have tried it at least once, according to the Substance Abuse and Mental Health Services Administration (SAMHSA).

Inhaling the compressed gas—whether from chargers, a whipped cream canister, or a nitrous tank—results in a short high that can last anywhere from several seconds to several minutes. While some states have attempted to regulate inhalant use through laws, experts say the use o

(continued from the previous page)

whippets and Whip-It! brand canisters are mostly ignored by authorities and left unregulated. But just because it is a legal high doesn't make it any less dangerous. Actress Demi Moore was reportedly using whippets shortly before she was rushed to the hospital in January 2012. Benjamin Collen, a nineteen-year-old Illinois college student, died from asphyxiation from nitrous oxide in 2008; he was found in a fraternity house surrounded by Whip-It! chargers.

After a substantial drop in popularity lasting several decades, poppers enjoyed a revival during the 1990s rave scene as a dance floor drug of choice and became a staple, alongside MDMA (or ecstasy) and LSD. Rave and electronic dance music enthusiasts used poppers for their "rush," as the high enhanced the experience of dancing to pulsating music and lights. While inhalants were once traditionally associated with the dentist's chair and labor ward, they are now popular at music festivals for their similarity in effects to hard drugs, but with much shorter (five- to ten-minute-long) durations. Other enticing features include their cheap price and legal status—several doses can be bought legally for a few dollars.

LEGAL ACTION

Doctors have witnessed and documented some cases in which inhalants contributed to or caused negative health effects or death. However, it has proven difficult to substantiate these claims through the legal system because of the everyday chemical makeup—and legality—of the substances and their components. Over the years, legislation has been abandoned in at least three American states after difficulty identifying the offending additives. Working with the companies that produce these products has led to mixed results in the prevention process as well.

One thing that has proven helpful has been compulsory labeling, which makes unsafe products—and their components—easier to identify before they're used. While this course of action alone does nothing to restrain buyers from purchasing these products with the intent to abuse them, it does expose their harmful ingredients to the appropriate authoritative bodies. Some success has also been found when companies have agreed or chosen to replace harmful components with safer substances. While some ethically minded companies have chosen to go this route on their own, another major driver here has come from new standards being set forth in legislation.

AMPED ON AMMONIA

In 2005, the *Florida Times-Union* exposed a group of National Football League (NFL) and college-level football players who were openly sniffing cartridges of ammonia on the sidelines before and during game play. Hundreds of players were witnessed casually raising the white cartridges to their noses during in-season games, including former Green Bay quarterback Brett Favre and the New York Giants' Michael Strahan, a twelve-year veteran and Pro Bowl winner. As the

(continued on the next page)

(continued from the previous page)

inhalant is not illegal nor against the rules of either the NFL or the National Collegiate Athletic Association (NCAA), Strahan did not hesitate to tell reporter Mike Freeman that he used one before each game. Inhalants are commonplace; in fact, Strahan says he would estimate between 70 to 80 percent of the NFL uses them. Both Peyton Manning and Tom Brady have admitted to using them as well. In fact, Brady has stated, "We all do it. It's kind of a receiver and quarterback thing."

Designed to revive an unconscious player, its current use as a performance enhancer is not what the company intended, as affirmed by a company spokesperson. They are typically used by first-aid personnel to "wake up" a player who has been hit and lost consciousness on the field. However, on some teams, members of the staff are handing out the

cartridges to players. In some cases, the ammonia was being mixed with an unknown liquid before being inhaled; players would not comment on this practice or admit what the liquid was. Inhalants are not banned in football, although they are banned in other professional sports, such as boxing.

Not all players are willing to risk their health for the rush.

Former Giants defensive end Michael Strahan has spoken openly about the widespread use and abuse of ammonia cartridges by NFL players.

Ty Warren, a former defensive lineman for the New England Patriots, said he did not use the cartridges because he was concerned about possible health effects. "I have enough things to worry about with playing football than using a lot of these things and having a tumor grow in my head," he reasoned. In reality, the health risks typically involve damage to the respiratory system, especially with players who use a large number of cartridges over a long period of time. Strahan admits he should have considered the long-term effects ammonia could have on his body, but he said, "To be honest, I worry more about all of the hits [I've taken] and the toll the violence [took] on my body than the ammonia."

Of course, changing drug standards or labels is not always a success. While nitrous oxide (also known as laughing gas) was banned in the United Kingdom in 2015 and remains illegal under the 2016 Psychoactive Substances Act, it is still the second most popular drug just after cannabis, as it remains a legal component of both culinary and medicinal tools—despite also being an element of jet fuel! In 2016, the British government presented statistics showing that more than 350,000 people ages sixteen to twenty-four admitted to using nitrous oxide in the past year. Here as well, the question of who is at fault comes into play. With most illegal drugs, there is a dealer. But when the "dealer" is a massive corporation that is not actively engaged in breaking any laws, who is at fault, and who should face the consequences of potential jail time?

CHAPTER 2

IDENTIFYING ABUSE

While inhalants may still enjoy a legal status when used on their own, young people often choose to take them alongside illegal drugs like MDMA. Though it remains uncommon, repeated use of inhalants can lead to addiction. Substance abuse disorder (SUD) is identified by the development of health problems and a failure to meet responsibilities at work, at school, or at home. The signs of abuse are subtler with inhalants than with many other drugs because the effects are experienced rapidly and also disappear quickly, with only small amounts of a substance required to achieve these results. Also, the products involved are typically legal and thus less conspicuous to purchase and store.

THINGS TO LOOK FOR

There are some signs to watch for if you think you or someone you know may be a possible inhalant abuser. A basic sign that one could easily miss (or misunderstand) is the large-scale storage

If you've noticed a friend becoming withdrawn and secretive about her personal space, and if you notice she stocks large amounts of household products, she could be hiding an addiction to inhalants.

of household products typically used as inhalants, especially in unusual or personal places such as under-bed storage. This is a tricky one in today's age, with the advent of Costco, couponing, and other bulk shopping destinations; just because your friend's parents store thirty bottles of cleaning solution and spray deodorant on shelves in their basement doesn't mean he or she is secretly living in a family of huffers—they may just love a good deal. However, if you find a closet filled with empty paint or solvent containers, or many of them seem to go missing or be hidden away, this could be indicative of SUD.

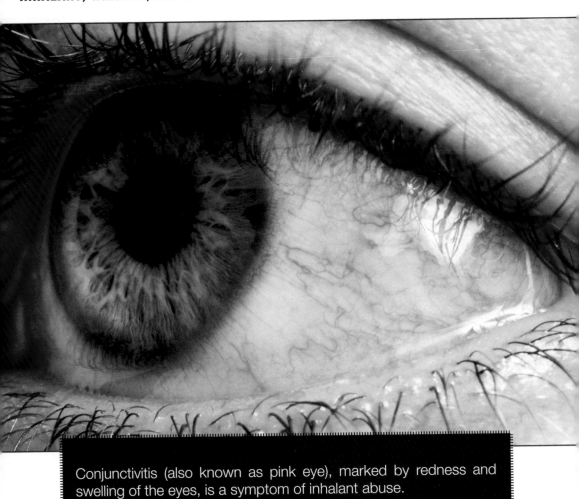

Conjunctivitis (also known as pink eye), marked by redness and swelling of the eyes, is a symptom of inhalant abuse.

There are also physical signs that one can look for, such as odor on the breath, skin, and clothing; stains, paint, or glitter on skin and clothing; and chemical-soaked rags or clothing. You may notice burns or frostbite of the face, especially around the mouth and nose. If a person has just used inhalants, he or she can appear drunk or dazed, with a disoriented appearance. You may also notice slurred speech, inattentiveness, lack of coordination, and irritability. With heavier abuse, you may detect loss of hygiene, weight, or energy; nosebleeds; conjunctivitis or swelling and redness of the eyes; muscle weakness; nausea; apathy; poor appetite; and gastrointestinal complaints (or a combination of a few of these symptoms). There is also a high correlation here with mood, anxiety, and personality disorders.

HUFFER'S RASH

Traditionally, what is known as "glue sniffer's rash" or "huffer's rash" refers to oral and nasal ulcerations, or an observable rash around the mouth of the inhalant abuser. Sometimes, trace elements of the product itself can be seen around the mouth and nose. This comes from holding a cloth saturated with the product to one's nose and/or mouth for a prolonged period and inhaling. Most inhalants contain volatile substances (like chloroform, butane, propane, acetone, toluene, and many halogenated hydrocarbons) but are free of large quantities of toxic components. But whether toxic or not, these chemicals are obviously not meant for direct contact with the skin and certainly not for extended periods of time or so close to one's orifices.

With skin exposure to solvents, nonspecific irritation is common and can progress to contact dermatitis with continued exposure. Drying, cracking, pitting, and lesions are also fairly common in those who repeatedly huff or abuse inhalants. As mentioned above, volatile solvent abusers (VSA) may have obvious paint, shoeshine, or solvent stains on their clothes or skin, particularly on the skin surrounding the nose and mouth. This can appear as a metallic circular area surrounding these two parts of the face. Nonfreezing cold injury may also be seen on or near the face when inhalers are intentionally releasing liquid hydrocarbon propellants, which cool as

PREVENTION IS THE BEST STRATEGY

Using inhalants may provide a legal, cheap, and quick high if it's done once—but for many, once is not enough. One woman, Debbie Goldman, began using whippets in law school and continued the habit for years while also working at a high-profile law firm. Going through dozens of chargers a day, her appetite for whippets became insatiable. Surely, she must have exhibited some of the signs of SUD—at her peak, she was using 240

Chargers used for whippets are readily available and cheap, which has fueled levels of addiction to these drugs.

chargers a night, after which her whole body would go numb and she would fall asleep. One would suspect that whether or not she confined this behavior to her own home or brought it into work with her, someone would have commented on the drug paraphernalia, or at the very least on the amount of whipped cream she had been "consuming." Sadly, no one intervened and one morning she woke up to find her legs had gone numb and she could not walk. She required six months of intensive physical therapy and now speaks out to prevent others from taking up the drug—and to gain the notice of officials. In 2012, she told *ABC News* that she believes whippets are addictive and they "should not be accessible like they are."

If you want to help avoid more horror stories involving inhalants, prevention is seen as the most effective strategy for combatting this type of drug abuse. As preteens are the most at-risk demographic, in-school prevention education must begin as early as possible for it to have any positive effects on those who have experienced it. Many people hear about marijuana, heroin, alcohol, and cocaine when learning about dangerous mind-altering drugs and chemicals, but inhalants are often overlooked both by parents and school programs. Prevention is only effective when it is community based, meaning it involves family, peers, schools, and retailers.

MYTHS AND FACTS

MYTH: Because inhalants are legal, they are less likely to kill me than other, illegal drugs.

FACT: Alcohol is also legal to consume, and yet it contributes to approximately 88,000 deaths per year in the United States alone, according to the Centers for Disease Control and Prevention (CDC). On the flip side, the CDC recorded an estimated 64,000 deaths from all known illegal drug overdoses in 2016—with just over 15,000 coming from heroin and 10,000 from cocaine. Just because a substance is legal does not make it safer.

MYTH: The fumes from inhalants pass through my body so quickly that there is no time for short-term effects, let alone prolonged effects.

FACT: Inhalants produce noticeable short-term effects, whose appearance can be similar to those from alcohol use—such as slurred speech, lack of coordination, dizziness, and light-headedness. Other long-term health effects include liver and kidney damage, bone marrow damage, and motor, cognitive, and sensory deficits.

MYTH: While whippets and other inhalants are primarily a drug of choice for preteens, only older people use poppers, so as a young adult I don't have to worry about exposure to them and neither do my friends.

FACT: Despite their primary function and expected effects, poppers have gained some clout among young people at music festivals and through articles featuring the drug on popular websites like the Tangential and Dazed Digital. With the internet—and access to YouTube tutorials—potential sources of peer pressure have become a lot more diverse.

CHAPTER 3

MEDICAL EFFECTS

Besides behavioral signs and skin-deep physical effects such as huffer's rash, there are a number of even more sinister effects that can appear after only limited exposure with the chemicals in question. These short-term effects can cause permanent damage, even changing the makeup of the abuser's anatomy—particularly by damaging cellular development in the brain. Literally speaking, inhaling chemical solvents will cause cells in your brain to die; these cells will not grow back.

With consequences as dire as cell death currently being left out of the conversation, it is not surprising that these products remain on supermarket shelves and their abuse remains legal. But despite a dearth of extended studies focused on inhalants and their effects, doctors have been able to pull together some findings after years of observing their use and abuse. While not all of these findings are conclusive, they are what we have to go on for now—at least until further research can be found necessary, funded, and conducted.

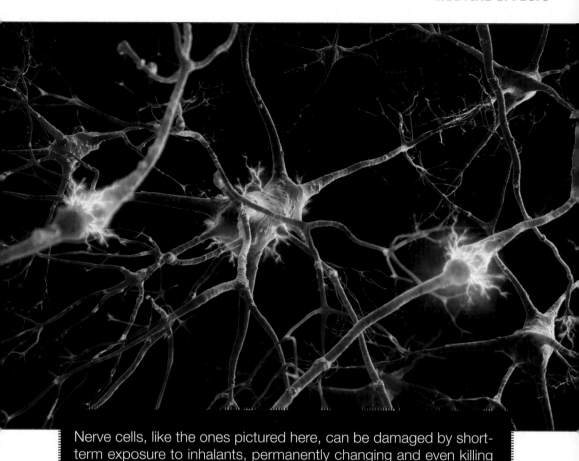

Nerve cells, like the ones pictured here, can be damaged by short-term exposure to inhalants, permanently changing and even killing key elements of the brain and central nervous system.

SHORT-TERM EFFECTS ON THE BRAIN AND BODY

Inhalants primarily affect the central nervous system by slowing brain activity down. Short-term effects of inhalant use are similar to those observed from alcohol use, including slurred or distorted speech, lack of coordination or body movement control, euphoria (which is the feeling of being "high"), dizziness, light-headedness, hallucinations, and delusions. Initial effects of inhalants can also be compared to those of anesthetics, including hallucinations, generalized depression, disorientation, and drowsiness or sleep

23

A common effect of inhaling is dizziness or light-headedness, which can kick in just seconds or minutes after using the drug. If your friend seems drowsy and disoriented, stay with her—and don't let her drive.

(which kicks in anywhere from seconds to minutes after use).

Repeated inhalations can lead to less self-control and self-consciousness, vomiting, drowsiness, and headache. In addition to freezing and burning of the face, some kinds of inhalants can also have the same effects on the upper aerodigestive tract. This includes the organs and tissues of the respiratory tract (including the sinuses and windpipe) and the upper digestive tract (including lips, mouth, tongue, and esophagus). These ulcers and burns would make using the windpipe and esophagus quite painful, affecting speech, breathing, and consumption of both liquids and solids. This symptom could lead to another physical effect: weight loss. Over time, the inhalant abuser may lose a significant amount of body weight.

While drugs are often blamed for errors in judgment, it is ultimately the participants' decision to engage with the drug,

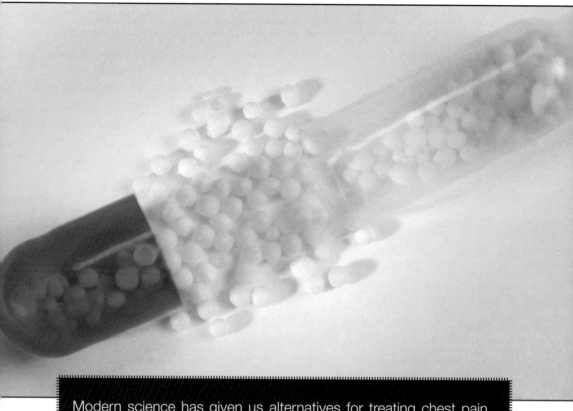

Modern science has given us alternatives for treating chest pain, such as this pill, Monicor, which is derived from nitrates but not easily abused as an inhalant.

knowing its mind-altering nature beforehand. Unfortunately, every scenario is not this cut and dry—sometimes drugs are slipped into drinks and taken involuntarily. Nitrates in particular, which can still be prescribed to treat chest pain on occasion, expand and relax blood vessels—and thus, are misused for sexual pleasure. While some users of poppers remain in control and take responsibility for their behavior and their partner's well-being, as with the addition of anything that can change one's mental state, one must be careful. Without a degree of attentiveness, abuse of poppers can lead to unsafe or risky sexual practices, such as intercourse without protection, engaging in sex acts with strangers or without discussion of one's partner's sexual health status, or with multiple partners over a short period of time. Of course, none of these behaviors will inherently cause sexually transmitted infections (STIs), but they are known to increase their likelihood—and can heighten the risk of contracting human immunodeficiency virus (HIV) and hepatitis as a result.

DOCTORS ABUSE LAUGHING GAS

You wouldn't expect your trusted doctor to be caught abusing the drugs he or she has been entrusted to write prescriptions for, let alone stealing the very tools he or she needs to make you more comfortable and feel better. Unfortunately, that is exactly what Dr. Jonathan Chahal was charged with doing while working at the Ormskirk and District General Hospital in the UK during the summer of 2007. The thirty-three-year-old doctor inhaled a medical anesthetic called Entonox, which is often administered in childbirth to ease pain, from a gas canister on at least four occasions. He also persuaded seven nurses to join him, describing their behavior as an "Entonox party" while on duty as a senior officer for the children's accident and emergency (A&E) ward. He could also be heard giggling while working and told colleagues that the drug was "fun" and "made you feel floaty."

A General Medical Council hearing convened, during which the panel ruled that Chahal's behavior put his patients in potential danger; while not

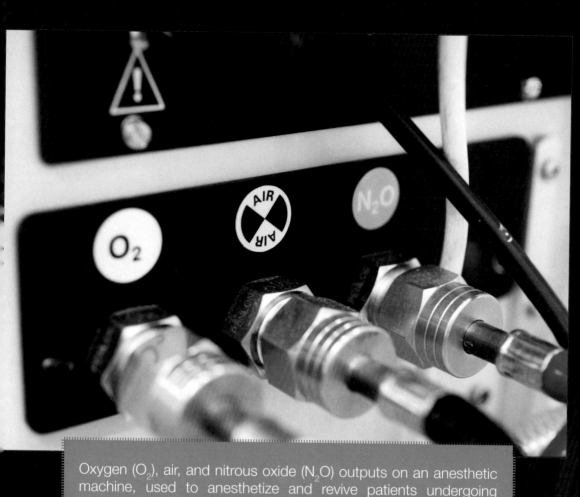

Oxygen (O_2), air, and nitrous oxide (N_2O) outputs on an anesthetic machine, used to anesthetize and revive patients undergoing surgery in hospitals.

illegal, using Entonox while working in an emergency pediatric department, where patients' conditions change rapidly, could impair function essential to one's work. Chahal acknowledged that he was "incredibly foolish" and it was fortunate that he had not harmed any of his patients. Although the probability that Chahal would repeat his behavior was deemed low, the chairman acknowledged that the panel "must send a message to the profession and to the public that [his] actions were wholly unacceptable." Ultimately, Chahal lost his job due to the allegations.

LONG-TERM HEALTH EFFECTS

Chronic abuse of inhalants can lead to serious and often irreversible health effects. In fact, long-term use has resulted in brainstem dysfunction and motor, cognitive, and sensory deficits. Signs include irritability, tremor, ataxia (lack of muscle coordination), nystagmus (uncontrolled eye movements), decreased vision, and deafness. Other long-term health effects include liver and kidney damage, hearing loss, bone marrow damage, loss of coordination and limb spasms caused by nerve damage, delayed behavioral development, and brain damage—specifically from cutting off the flow of oxygen to the brain.

Women who have been exposed to solvents have been known to have more menstrual disorders, and for those who abuse inhalants, preeclampsia (high blood pressure, fluid retention, and protein in the urine) and spontaneous abortions are more common. The inhalants can even affect the fetus with what is known as "fetal solvent syndrome." The initial findings for this term come from a 1999 study that concluded that exposure to solvents during pregnancy increased the risk of major fetal malformations, especially in women who were symptomatic. These malformations involved many different organs and organ systems, including the heart and central nervous system. Those who were exposed for seven months or longer were also more likely to have fetal distress in labor and lower birth weights in their infants overall. The study concluded that exposure to such solvents should be reduced as much as possible during pregnancy, particularly in those who were symptomatic. Therefore, if pregnant women who are naturally exposed to solvents are in danger, then inhalant abusers are even more at risk.

Overdosing from inhalants is a possible outcome for those who choose to abuse. In general, an "overdose" is defined as "a toxic reaction resulting in serious symptoms, damage, and even death." Symptoms of overdose from inhalant abuse include seizures and coma, sudden sniffing death (in which one's heart just stops), and death from suffocation, which is the inability to breathe, resulting from using a bag to inhale. Solvents and sprays contain concentrated, active chemical ingredients that are not meant for physical consumption. Unfortunately, inhalant use is not usually detectable from a routine urine screening, and the screening is rarely performed by health care providers, though this may be one of the most valuable tools in inhalant abuse detection—and thus prevention.

CHAPTER 4

WHO IS AFFECTED?

The appearance of an inhalant user may not be what you'd expect when stereotyping a "drug user." The National Survey on Drug Use and Health conducted in 2010 found that 68 percent of inhalant abusers in the United States are under eighteen years old. According to a 2013 UK government study, 6.1 percent of those ages sixteen to twenty-four had taken the drug just in the last year. In 2011, 7 percent of eighth graders reported use, with that number dropping as the grade level increased. About 4.5 percent of tenth graders and 3.2 percent of twelfth graders also reported inhalant use.

But even the perception of inhalants as "kids' drugs" (i.e., "glue sniffers") deserves some amount of consideration and reassessment. This is a class of drugs shared by suburban and rural preteens in America, First Nations communities in Canada, and people undergoing famine in developing countries.

The majority of inhalant abusers in the United States are under eighteen, with a higher rate of abuse among younger teens.

There is not one face of the inhalant user, nor is there one reason for inhaling.

WHY SNIFF?

Chances are, depending on whom you ask, you would get a very different answer to the question of why that person first tried inhalants. Inhalants are used for different reasons in different places. Abuse has been found more commonly among school dropouts, those who have been physically or sexually abused or neglected, the incarcerated and homeless, and Native American and Aboriginal communities. In fact, it is more prevalent in rural and isolated communities with higher rates of unemployment, poverty, and violence than in large cities or suburban areas. There isn't one consistent reason that would tie these groups to one another or drive them all to seek brief spells of euphoria, except perhaps a reason that many drug users find themselves drawn to—as a form of escapism. There are also the obvious external factors, which include that inhalants are cheap and legal to purchase, and don't require any involvement with drug dealers or paraphernalia to acquire and use.

Among younger users, studies have shown that if their friends and peers are using inhalants, they are more likely to use them as well. Teenagers report using inhalants at their friends' homes and on school property. There is also a strong correlation with less supportive families, poor school performance, criminal behavior, social maladjustment, poor self-esteem and suicidal ideation, psychiatric conditions, abuse of other substances, and heightened substance abuse amongs family and peers. Of course, not everyone is meant to relate to all of these factors; they are just some of the most common denominators associated with inhalant abuse.

Strikingly though, there is also a strong correlation between inhalants and poverty, hunger, illness, low education levels, unemployment, boredom, and feelings of hopelessness. Higher rates of inhalant abuse among some Aboriginal populations—in Canada in particular, among Inuit and First Nations communities— are due to socioeconomic status and are not inherent to ethnicity. Similarly, in parts of the developing world, inhalants are used primarily to relieve pain due to hunger. After a bit of thought, it might not be so surprising that the same thing that alleviates boredom and angst in a comparatively privileged teenager would also be an effective escape for anyone else needing a bit of escape—including the homeless or undernourished populations of this world.

REAL STORIES: LOS ANGELES

Sometimes, drug abuse appears more like a plot in a movie than real life. In November 2013, Jorge Leonardo Sanchez led Los Angeles police on a car chase that ended with the twenty-four-year-old Sanchez inhaling a large quantity of nitrous oxide from balloons in the driver's seat of his car while under police surveillance. At the scene, the man's father told reporters that Sanchez "had problems in the past with nitrous oxide," the inhalant typically known as laughing gas. According to court records, Sanchez's history includes possession of nitrous oxide in 2009, domestic battery, trespassing, and disturbing the peace.

Los Angeles saw a surge and subsequent crackdown on nitrous oxide in 2013, though it remains a popular drug in California today. On March 22, 2013, LA County Sheriff's officials announced Operation No Laughing Matter, which saw law enforcement targeting more than twelve nitrous oxide "distribution centers," mostly auto shops where tanks meant for vehicles were ending up at raves and parties around the city. According to the US Attorney's Office, authorities served twenty-six search warrants on

(continued on the next page)

(continued from the previous page)

seventeen businesses and nine delivery vehicles as part of the raid. Prosecutors alleged they were "misbranding" nitrous oxide, as they were distributing it for personal use without prescription or proper warning labels. The defendants faced a year behind bars and fines of $100,000.

With this background information in mind, one would suspect Sanchez may have been attempting to hide the "evidence" of another illegally obtained nitrous oxide tank, as if inhaling all of the contents of the tank while under police surveillance would remove all culpability. But when we recall that laughing gas does not show up on a urine or toxicology report (and that Sanchez was initially pulled over on suspicion of drunk driving), perhaps his behavior becomes clearer after all.

While the Los Angeles Police Department ran a campaign to crack down on nitrous oxide abuse in 2013, many US cities have done nothing to resolve the abuse of inhalants within their borders.

THE ANTI-HOLLYWOOD DRUG

There is a strong case to be made for a two-fold reason why the pervasiveness of inhalant use has largely been left out of media reports—at least when compared with other drugs like cocaine, whose use has been picked apart and even glamorized by both the primetime news and paparazzi.

First, inhalants are primarily used as household products. These products are easy for young people to get their hands on, and any public discussion of them bears the risk of teaching a new crop of preteens how to locate and abuse everyday products suitable for inhaling. (Of course, the flip side of this is that with less information, potential abusers could inhale even more dangerous or toxic solvents and end up in an even worse situation than if they had been more informed.)

The second reason takes a look at demographics. Inhalant use is most prevalent in poor communities, among

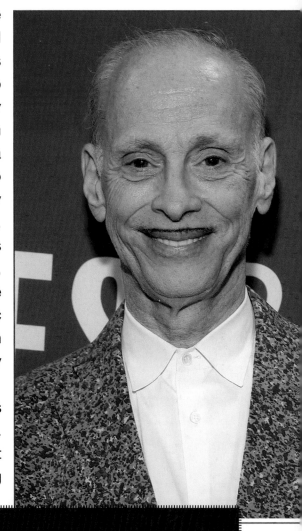

Filmmaker and artist John Waters has spoken openly about his use of poppers.

the incarcerated and homeless, and among young teenagers living in rural environments. It is perceived as a drug for people with poor self-esteem, bad habits, and criminal behavior. But this is not entirely true. Many celebrities, in addition to professional athletes, have used or abused the drug, including writer and director John Waters. In his live show "This Filthy World," Waters admitted that while he has given up most of the drugs he took in his youth, he still occasionally does poppers for their quick rush. In fact, one of his own art pieces is a gigantic bottle of Rush, a brand of poppers. As Waters tells it, the owner of the company sent him a lifetime supply of the poppers, which he keeps in his freezer, with the constant fear that someone will come over, have a look in his freezer, and think he's hooked. Several other celebrities have also been linked to whippets, including Demi Moore, who went to rehab after using the drug, and Steve-O (from MTV's *Jackass*), who was allegedly addicted to them. But despite their use among celebrities, few people talk about the prevalence and dangers of these drugs. Inhalant abuse might always be relegated to the fringes—and people who are addicted to inhalants might continue to suffer in silence—if it is not talked about more openly.

CHAPTER 5

PRACTICAL ADVICE

While it is true that inhalants attract an array of users, preteens and young adults are among the highest affected demographic. For this reason, family, peers, teachers, and counselors should be made aware of the signs of inhalant abuse and how to refer at-risk children and young adults for help. Obviously, preventative measures are the most effective at curbing the use of inhalants in the long run, but for those currently abusing, seeking treatment is incredibly important for overcoming any dependence on the substance.

SEEKING TREATMENT

Widespread screening and early referrals to treatment programs have shown significant improvements in drug users' lives. But what does treatment of inhalant addiction really look like? While treatment isn't available for withdrawal or acute intoxication

Speaking with a therapist is a key part of any treatment plan for inhalant abuse, particularly given its high rate of comorbidity with mood disorders and other mental illnesses.

(meaning those currently experiencing the short-term effects of inhaling) aside from vigilant and supportive care, long-term effects can be mitigated by or even prevented with early treatment. This treatment (i.e., rehabilitation and therapy) can effectively help abusers quit using inhalants altogether and, when approached holistically, prevent their recurrence.

COPING WITH WITHDRAWAL

When going through withdrawal, the inhalant user becomes the worst version of his or herself and has the potential to become even worse. And being a caregiver for someone undergoing inhalant withdrawal is difficult—it may even feel impossible. Just remember, nothing you do

(continued on the next page)

Breaking free from dependency on inhalants can feel like a daunting task, but it's one you don't need to face alone. Accept help from friends and family, or seek treatment in a rehabilitation center.

(continued from the previous page)

will ever be perfect, but just being physically present for your loved one in withdrawal is the best support you can provide.

Inhalant abusers should consult a doctor before quitting, or be guided through the withdrawal process at a drug treatment center. Teen recovery centers are available for adolescents. These programs provide detox, counseling, and recreational activities, and may permit students to complete schoolwork while participating in the program. If a concurrent mental or behavioral health condition is also present, detox at a dual diagnosis treatment center used to treating these multiple conditions could be very beneficial.

Withdrawal symptoms for inhalants generally present within the first twenty-four to forty-eight hours after the last use. Immediate symptoms include hand tremors, nausea, loss of appetite, sweating, problems sleeping, anxiety, irritability, and mood changes. In severe cases, the patient may suffer from seizures, hallucination, or psychosis. The duration and severity of withdrawal symptoms vary, but most people go through the worst of withdrawal in about a week. However, psychological symptoms, such as cravings and depression, can last a lot longer than physical symptoms. Some inhalant users have stated that they suffered from psychological withdrawal for many months after quitting, and long after their physical symptoms disappeared.

If you are searching for treatment for yourself or a friend, it is important that the program includes peer-to-patient advocacy and development of patients' strengths and skills. Building a network of strong peers around yourself or your friend, who can be turned to as models for behavior and appropriate positioning in the community, can be incredibly helpful for recovery from inhalant abuse. Whether you are the abuser or the friend of an

While it may be difficult to let your family and friends know that you are hurting, just telling someone who truly cares about you what you are going through can help start the process toward recovery.

abuser, you cannot fix this on your own. Advocates know that they are being depended upon and are choosing to do this voluntarily; they are there to help—let them lend you their support. Equally important, though, is knowing your own strengths and what you can do on your own. While everyone has limits, everyone also has their own set of skills and strengths to bring to the table.

Treatment for addiction should also involve an element of therapy. Cognitive behavioral therapy (CBT) helps patients recognize, avoid, and deal with situations in which they may be more likely to use drugs. Family therapy and both parental reinforcement and enforcement of appropriate behavior is considered another key component of therapy. However, in some communities, drug abuse can be either denied or normalized in unhealthy ways. For obvious reasons, if you are part of a community where this is the case, then seeking family therapy to help you cope may not be appropriate—although it may be helpful to explore once your addiction has been curbed. It is also important to treat co-current conditions, other dependencies, and the presence of mental and physical disorders. Inhalant abuse has a strong correlation with low self-esteem, boredom, feelings of loneliness, and even depression and suicidal ideation. If you aren't addressing any coexisting issues as part of your treatment plan, your chances of success are not as good as they would be with more comprehensive treatment.

TEN GREAT QUESTIONS
TO ASK A THERAPIST

1. Is addiction to inhalants physical or mental?

2. My friends can go to parties and just inhale one or two canisters, but I have to go through thirty or more in a night. It's like once I start, I can't stop. Why do some people become addicted to poppers while others don't?

3. A photo of me using inhalants was circulated online, and now I'm too ashamed to face people at school and in my community who have found out that I'm a potential drug abuser. What can I do?

4. As a teenager and someone under eighteen years old, can I get treatment for drug abuse without my parents knowing?

5. Are certain inhalants worse for you than others?

6. I started doing whippets because my friends told me they were cheap and legal. Now I know they might be killing my brain cells, but if I stop taking them won't I just get addicted to something else—potentially, worse—instead?

7. I can't avoid going into the storage room in my parents' basement forever. How will I know I'm ready to return to triggering places?

8. I've tried quitting before, but so far I always end up relapsing. What are some new things I can try to help make it stick this time?

9. I saw my favorite NFL players inhaling drugs on the sidelines this season. Why does everyone say inhaling ammonia is bad for you if athletes—some of the world's healthiest people—are choosing to do it as a way of prepping for games?

10. My friends all use inhalants and don't see a problem with it. How can I spend time with them without feeling pressured to join in or end up falling back on old habits?

CHAPTER 6

GETTING A FRESH START

Recovering from addiction and drug abuse is not an easy process for anyone. At this stage, you have attempted to stop using inhalants and perhaps you have succeeded, either by entering a treatment facility or attempting to quit on your own or with the support of family, friends, and your community (or all of the above!). But just because you've stopped doesn't mean the journey to sobriety ends there.

As with any drug, there is a very real chance of sliding back into old habits. That is why it is so important for you to establish good habits and remove bad ones as you move forward and find motivational incentives—like rewards for positive behaviors—for staying drug-free. And remember, you shouldn't have to do any of this on your own. If they're able to, let your family and friends be of service to you and accept the support and love they send your way.

It can be hard to imagine what a sober lifestyle might feel like, but try to keep a positive attitude and remember to reward yourself as you progress.

ONGOING TREATMENT

Maybe you have come to the end of your treatment inside the rehab center or treatment facility, and now it is time to proceed to the next step in your recovery plan. For some, this means going home—back into the environment where they first started abusing inhalants. For others, this may involve moving into a halfway home or another facility where they will be afforded more freedom than they had in rehab, without having quite as much time on their hands as they might have had before.

You will probably still need to find a practicing psychologist or psychiatrist and maintain ongoing therapy, either on your own or with family support. Inhalant abuse has a high comorbidity with mental illness (such as anxiety and depression) and abuse of other substances; it will be important to keep an eye on these diagnoses as well. Also, while teen recovery centers may have groups focused on issues specific to teen drug abuse, such as improving self-esteem and resisting peer pressure, it can be difficult to follow through with what one has learned back in the outside world.

WHERE TO GO?

Inspirations for Youth and Families is a residential treatment center for teens (ages thirteen to eighteen) and their families geared toward treating teen drug and alcohol addiction as well as any accompanying mental or behavioral issues. Academics, therapy, and family involvement are all part of Inspirations' treatment approach. Patients there work toward acquiring necessary life skills and personal goals, while promoting accountability and learning healthy decision making.

Other focal points include treatment based on repairing personal and family dysfunction through learned behaviors, an on-site school program for teens to prepare them for high school graduation and university acceptance, and technical training toward placement in a career. As residents, teens live in gender-specific dorms with a four-to-one ratio of teens to staff around the clock. Teens do chores and are never isolated; in fact, taking part in fun (and sober) activities like concerts, movies, beach trips, and sporting events are considered essential at Inspiration.

One of the specific subsets of drugs treated at Inspirations is abuse of inhalants. On the Inspirations website (http://www.inspirationsyouth.com), there is a particularly helpful information page on the subject that offers statistics of use and abuse, and vocabulary related to inhalant abuse and drug addiction more generally. The facility uses a combination of family therapy, music and art therapy, psychotherapy, and recreational therapy to treat inhalant abuse, as well as making use of behavioral treatment programs such as dual-diagnosis, cognitive behavioral development, recreational, music, art, and trauma therapy, and its nationally renowned Teen Intervention Program.

One of the benefits of entering a treatment facility is the support of a peer group who knows what you're going through—they've committed themselves to change as well.

DIY: THINGS YOU CAN MANAGE ON YOUR OWN

Transitioning back into the community will depend a great deal on what your support system looks like. In an ideal world, you would have friends and family who will help and love you to fall back on, and an empathetic, tight-knit community that understands and will do their best not to judge or trigger you. Having a strong support network in place can really help you through the recovery process. But most people don't live in an ideal world and will need to be ready to fight against relapsing.

One thing you can do on your own to stop from sliding back into abuse is to try to avoid known triggers. Triggers are things that remind you of dangerous or painful situations or memories that can cause you to feel alarmed or even jump-start your desire to use. Do not spend time with friends who are still using, avoid stores where you would normally purchase substances and places where you would usually inhale, and discard any drug paraphernalia you may still have from before you sought treatment.

You can't live in a bubble forever, and eventually you'll have to learn some ways of coping with reality that do not involve avoidance. Besides therapy, some people find that participating in alternative treatments improve their mental, physical, and spiritual well-being in ways that help them stay positive and avoid drugs. Yoga and meditation have shown positive results for some and are good ways of relieving stress in general. Exercise in general can also improve mood—and get your blood flowing without drugs. Go for a walk, a hike, or a swim if you can. Sometimes just getting outside of your known environment can do the trick. Joining a community-organized sports team,

Yoga and other forms of exercise can help you stay focused on rehabilitation since they can act as natural mood enhancers and are proven forms of stress release.

a club during or after school, or doing something creative like painting or playing an instrument could help. You may even find that some of these new habits help combat any concurrent issues of a psychological or mood-based nature. Get yourself stimulated if you are bored, restless, or feeling depressed. There are thousands of things out there to enjoy—reading, writing, knitting, woodworking, learning to code, learning a language… and the list goes on. Just remember, you can only improve if you are willing to make some lifestyle changes on your own and count every little step toward doing so.

GLOSSARY

ADDICTION The compulsive need for and use of a habit-forming substance known to be harmful.

ADVOCACY The act of supporting a person or a cause.

AEROSOL A substance dispensed from a pressurized container as a fine solid or liquid particles in gas.

ANGINA A heart condition that causes severe chest pains and shortness of breath.

ARTERIES Vessels that carry blood from the heart through the body.

COGNITIVE Related to conscious intellectual activity, such as thinking, reasoning, and remembering.

COMORBIDITY Two or more medical conditions existing at the same time but independently within the same body.

CONCURRENT Working at the same time or together.

CONJUNCTIVITIS Commonly called pink eye; inflammation marked by pinkness or redness of the eye, in conjunction with itching, burning, and irritation.

DELUSION A persistent and false belief regarding the self (or others) that is sustained despite evidence that shows its falsehood.

EUPHORIA A feeling of extreme happiness.

GASTROINTESTINAL Describes anything involving the stomach and intestines.

HALLUCINATION A perception of objects or sounds (visual or auditory) with no basis in reality, commonly due to a disorder of the nervous system or as a symptom of drug use.

HYGIENE Conditions or practices conducive to the maintenance of health.

NITRATE A chemical compound that contains oxygen and nitrogen.

NITRITE Nitrous acid.

ORIFICE Any opening through which something may pass.

PARAPHERNALIA Equipment or accessories, particularly to do with drugs and drug use (e.g., needles, pipes, bongs, rolling papers).

PREVENTION The act of stopping or hindering something.

PSYCHOACTIVE Affecting the mind or behavior.

SOLVENT Anything that dissolves or can dissolve when in contact with water.

TOXIC Containing poisonous material capable of serious physical harm and/or death.

TRIGGER One thing that sets something else off, as in initiating a process or reaction.

FOR MORE INFORMATION

Canadian Centre on Substance Use and Addiction (CCSA)
75 Albert Street, Suite 500
Ottawa, ON K1P 5E7
Canada
(613) 235-4048
Website: http://www.ccsa.ca
Twitter: @CCSACanada
YouTube: @CCSACCLAT

The Canadian Centre on Substance Use and Addiction was created by the government to provide national leadership to address substance use in Canada. It provides national guidance to decision makers by harnessing the power of research, curating knowledge, and bringing together diverse perspectives.

Drug Free Kids Canada
Corus Quay
25 Dockside Drive
Toronto, ON M5A 0B5
Canada
(416) 479-6972
Website: https://www.drugfreekidscanada.org
Facebook: @DrugFreeKidsCanada
Twitter: @DrugFreeKidsCda
YouTube: @DrugFreeCanada

Drug Free Kids Canada maintains a comprehensive online space designed for parents to learn about drugs and teen drug abuse and to get helpful parenting tips. It works with advertising agencies and media partners to create drug education/prevention messages to provide parents with the tools they need to talk to their kids.

Elk River Treatment Program
500 Governors Drive SW
Huntsville, AL 3501
(866) 906-8336
Website: https://elkrivertreatment.com
Facebook: @elkrivertreatment
Twitter: @elkriverprogram
YouTube: @ertp4teens
Elk River Treatment Program is a residential teen treatment center focused on providing the highest quality professional care and teen rehabilitation available. It offers specialized programs for troubled teens dealing with behavioral and emotional issues, as well as drug rehab for teens struggling with addiction.

Inspirations for Youth and Families (IYF)
757 SE 17th Street
Fort Lauderdale, FL 33316
(888) 540-1437
Website: http://www.inspirationsyouth.com
Facebook: @inspirationsyouth
Twitter: @iyfteenrehab
Inspirations for Youth and Families is a nationally known adolescent drug and alcohol addiction and mental health rehabilitation facility. IYF is also a dual diagnosis facility specializing in the treatment of inhalants and huffing.

Muir Wood Trusted Teen Treatment
1733 Skillman Lane
Petaluma, CA 94952
(866) 705-0828
Website: https://muirwoodteen.com
Muir Wood is a world-renowned northern California treatment
    center for teens struggling with mental health, behavioral,
    and substance abuse issues. It offers information and
    resources on commonly abused substances, including
    inhalant abuse, residential inpatient treatment for teen boys in
    Sonoma County, and outpatient treatment for boys and girls
    in Marin County.

National Institute on Drug Abuse for Teens
Office of Science Policy and Communications
Public Information and Liaison Branch
6001 Executive Boulevard
Bethesda, MD 20892
Website: https://teens.drugabuse.gov
Facebook and YouTube: @NIDANIH
Twitter: @NIDANews
The purpose of NIDA for Teens is to facilitate learning about the
    effects of drug use on the brain, body, and lives of teens,
    written specifically for a teen audience. The site is a project of
    the National Institute on Drug Abuse (NIDA), the National
    Institutes of Health (NIH), and the US Department of Health
    and Human Services.

New Beginnings Drug & Alcohol Rehabilitation
(855) 338-6709
Website: http://www.newbeginningsdrugrehab.org

Facebook: @newbeginningsdrugrehab

Twitter: @NBDrugRehab

New Beginnings is an information-gathering website without bias, where one can search for rehabilitation centers and treatment methods. The idea behind New Beginnings is that there is a "right" recovery center out there for everyone, and it will help find the right center for you.

Partnership for Drug-Free Kids

352 Park Avenue South, 9th Floor

New York, NY 10010

(855) 378-4373

Website: https://drugfree.org

Facebook: @partnershipdrugfree

Twitter and Instagram: @thepartnership

YouTube: @drugfreechannel

The Partnership for Drug-Free Kids began as an organization committed to drug prevention through advertising and public service campaigns. For the past decade, it has focused on providing help that is not available to families elsewhere, including not only substance abuse prevention among kids but also treatment and help for those teens and young adults who are already struggling with drugs or drinking.

FOR FURTHER READING

entore, Michael, and Sara Becker. *Drug Use and Mental Health*. Broomall, PA: Mason Crest, 2017.

entore, Michael. *Drug Use and the Law*. Broomall, PA: Mason Crest, 2017.

entore, Michael. *Intervention and Recovery*. Broomall, PA: Mason Crest, 2017.

sherick, Joan. *Drug & Alcohol Related Health Issues*. Broomall, PA: Mason Crest Publishers, 2014.

ynn, Noa. *Inhalants & Solvents: Sniffing Disaster.* Broomall, PA: Mason Crest, 2014.

cKenzie, Precious. *Helping a Friend with a Drug Problem*. New York, NY: Rosen Publishing, 2017.

etersen, Christine. *Inhalants* (Dangerous Drugs). New York, NY: Cavendish Square, 2014.

oole, Hilary W. *Over-the-Counter Drugs*. Broomall, PA: Mason Crest, 2017.

rentzas, G. *The Truth About Inhalants* (Drugs & Consequences). New York, NY: Rosen Publishing, 2014.

ebman, Renée C. *Are You Doing Risky Things: Cutting, Bingeing, Snorting, and Other Dangers* (Got Issues?). Berkeley Heights,

BIBLIOGRAPHY

Adams, James G. *Emergency Medicine*. Philadelphia, PA: Saunders, 2008.

Barrett, David. "Laughing Gas Is Party Drug of Choice for Young People." *Telegraph*, July 25, 2013. http://www.telegraph .co.uk/news/uknews/crime/10202484/Laughing-gas-is -party-drug-of-choice-for-young-people.html.

Baydala, L. "Inhalant Abuse." *Paediatrics & Child Health*. September 2010, pp. 443–448. https://www.ncbi.nlm.nih .gov/pmc/articles/PMC2948777.

DeCapua, Melissa. "What You Should Know About Quitting Inhalants." Recovery.org, April 6, 2016. https://www.recovery .org/topics/quitting-inhalants.

Ebright, Olsen. "DUI Suspect Huffs on Balloons in Bizarre Standoff with Police." *NBC Los Angeles*, February 1, 2013. https://www.nbclosangeles.com/news/local/Police-Pursuit -Car-Chase-189404051.html.

Ewens, Hannah Rose. "The Secret History of Poppers." *Dazed Digital,* October 26, 2015. http://www.dazeddigital .com/artsandculture/article/27124/1/the-secret-history -of-poppers.

Freeman, Mike. "A Whiff of Trouble?" *Florida Times-Union*

Green, Rachel. "A Guide to Explaining Poppers to a Noob." *Tangential*, August 15, 2011. http://thetangential .com/2011/08/15/a-guide-to-explaining-poppers-to-a-noob.

Hicklin, Aaron. "John Waters Is Not a Poppers Pig." *Out*, May 18, 2010. https://www.out.com/news-commentary/2010/05/18 /john-waters-not-poppers-pig.

Karris, Ben Parker. "Why People Still Get Down on Whip-Its, Poppers, and Other Legal Highs." *The Kindland*, June 10, 2016. http://www.thekindland.com/products/why-people -still-get-down-on-whip-its-poppers-and-1619.

Khattak S., et al. "Fetal Solvent Syndrome." *JAMA*, May 1, 1999. https://www.ahcmedia.com/articles/41345-fetal -solvent-syndrome.

Levine, Barry, ed. *Principles of Forensic Toxicology.* 2nd ed. Washington, DC: AACC Press, 2003.

National Institute on Drug Abuse. "Inhalants." February 16, 2017. https://www.drugabuse.gov/publications/drugfacts /inhalants.

National Institute on Drug Abuse. "Overdose Death Rates." September 2017. https://www.drugabuse.gov/related-topics /trends-statistics/overdose-death-rates.

Rawlinson, Kevin, "Laughing Gas Still Illegal Despite Court Decisions, UK Government Says." *Guardian*, August 31, 2017. https://www.theguardian.com/society/2017/aug/31 /laughing-gas-still-illegal-despite-court-decisions -government-says.

Romero, Dennis. "Nitrous Oxide Bust Announced by LA Sheriff's Department." *LA Weekly*, March 22, 2013. http://www .laweekly.com/news/nitrous-oxide-bust-announced-by-la -sheriffs-department-4173650.

Rooks, Ashley. "What Is Inhalants Detox?" *Mental Help*, November 24, 2015. https://www.mentalhelp.net/articles /inhalants-detox.

Ross, Brian, and Megan Chuchmach. "Dangerous Teen Craze Whip-Its Making a Comeback?" *ABC News*, March 27, 2012. http://abcnews.go.com/Blotter/dangerous-teen-craze-whip -making-comeback/story?id=16006130.

Sparber, Max. "Searching for a Good Poppers Anecdote: John Waters at the Walker." *MinnPost*, July 13, 2011. https:// www.minnpost.com/max-about-town/2011/06/searching -good-poppers-anecdote-john-waters-walker.

Telegraph. "Doctor Inhaled Laughing Gas While on Duty at Children's Ward." July 13, 2009. http://www.telegraph.co.uk /news/uknews/5820136/Doctor-inhaled-laughing-gas-while -on-duty-at-childrens-ward.html.

Vinton, Nathaniel. "How Smelling Salts Have Been Used in the NFL, Including After Head Injuries." *Daily News*, June 15, 2016. http://www.nydailynews.com/sports/football/smelling -salts-nfl-head-injuries-article-1.2675345.

INDEX

ABOUT THE AUTHOR

Carolyn DeCarlo is a poet and fiction writer from Baltimore, Maryland, who now lives in New Zealand. She has volunteered in psychiatric wards of the Sheppard and Enoch Pratt Hospital in Towson, Maryland, and St. Elizabeth's Hospital in Washington, DC. She was also a mentor for the ASK Program, serving at-risk youth in the juvenile justice system of Washington, DC. She has a BA in English and psychology from Georgetown University and an MFA in creative writing from the University of Maryland, College Park. She has written several chapbooks, including *Green Place* (Enjoy Journal, 2015).

PHOTO CREDITS